# TIC-TAC-TOE
# MUSIC GAMES

## Reproducible Book Featuring Six Fun Activities for Kids

### BY KAREN HARRINGTON

**HAL•LEONARD®**
CORPORATION
7777 W. BLUEMOUND RD. P.O. BOX 13819 MILWAUKEE, WI 53213

# TIC-TAC-GAMES

## Suggestions for Playing the Games

1. Each **Tic-Tac-Game** may be played by any number of players. For each game, cut out the calling cards from the calling card sheet and place them in a bag for safekeeping. There are ten playing cards for each game. Reproduce the number of playing cards needed. The cards are numbered to make it easier to copy and distribute the cards evenly among the players. The cards may be laminated so they will be more durable. Players may wish to play two cards at the same time.

2. Divide the class into sections and choose a student leader for each group. Let the leader draw and call the cards. Each group can then play their own rounds of the game. You might wish to set up stations with a different game at each one. Groups can move to a different station after a certain number of rounds.

3. Keep a box of tokens to hand out. You can find bingo chips, plastic pieces, or tokens at variety stores. Students especially enjoy using small candies so they can eat the candy at the end of the game.

4. The games go fairly fast when players only need three in a row in any direction to win. Variations could be:
   1) cover the four corners
   2) cover the top, middle or bottom row
   3) black out or cover all squares

5. After playing a game several times, players may trade cards so they can find items on a different card.

# Suggestions and Additional Activities
## for the Individual Games

### TIC-TAC-SYMBOLS
1. Make a copy of the Master Sheet for each student for study before playing the game.
2. When first playing the game the teacher may name each symbol or draw it on the board.
3. When students are familiar with all symbols, the teacher may call just the definitions. The teacher may have one student identify the symbol to help the other players.
4. For a variation, players may take turns "acting out" the symbols. For instance, someone could choose to make a loud sound for the forte or clap four times for the time signature. Let their imaginations go.

### TIC-TAC-NOTES
1. The notes range from low "C" on the bass staff to high "C" on the treble staff. For players with lesser ability there are two cards that have no ledger line notes.
2. Using a large grand staff, review the names of the line notes, space notes and ledger line notes before playing the game.
3. For ear training, play the note on an instrument as it is named.
4. If there are students who have trouble naming the notes, place him next to a student helper.

### TIC-TAC-RHYTHM
1. For beginning students, hand out copies of the master sheet and review the rhythms before playing the game.
2. From the Master Sheet let the players clap or play the rhythms for others to identify.
3. Set the tempo by counting aloud. A metronome may be used.
4. Use the game as a dictation game. Tap the rhythms and ask students to write the rhythms they hear.

## TIC-TAC-INTERVALS

1. Make copies of the Master Sheet for the players. Review the intervals visually by observing lines and spaces between the intervals.
2. This game is particularly useful for melodic dictation.
    A) Sing or play the intervals and ask players to identify them from the Master Sheet or write them on a piece of manuscript paper.
    B) Ask the players to identify the intervals by quality.
3. For advanced players, reverse the direction of the intervals.

## TIC-TAC-KEYS

1. Make a copy of the Master Sheet for each student for study before playing the game.
2. For players who are not familiar with the key signatures, call the number of sharps or flats on the calling card and let a player identify the key. The players then cover the correct key.
3. For major key study, call just the major keys. For minor study, call the minor keys.
4. For ear training, play a short phrase or cadence in the key of the card called.

## TIC-TAC-TEMPOS

1. Make a copy of the Master Sheet for study before playing the game.
2. Have players play "Charades" by acting out the tempos.
3. For players who do not know the tempo words and their definitions, say the "Tempo Word" and the definition.
4. From the calling cards say only the definition and let players find the tempo word on their cards.

# TIC-TAC-SYMBOLS MASTER SHEET

| | | | | |
|---|---|---|---|---|
| Treble Clef | Bass Clef | Time Signature | Whole Note & Whole Rest | Half Note & Half Rest |
| Quarter Note & Quarter Rest | Eighth Note & Eighth Rest | Dotted Half Note | Staccato | Tie |
| Sharp | Flat | Natural | Bar Line | Fermata |
| Forte | Piano | Crescendo | Decrescendo or Diminuendo | Repeat |

**DIRECTIONS:** Place symbol calling cards face down and shuffle or mix. Give a "Tic-Tac-Symbols" game card and several tokens to each player. Draw calling cards one at a time. Call out the names of symbols, their meanings, or both; players find the corresponding symbol on their game cards. Place the calling card in the corresponding box on the master sheet. The winner is the first player to complete a row in any direction. The winner identifies himself by saying "Tic-Tac-Symbols" and he calls back the winning symbols for verification.

# TIC-TAC-SYMBOLS CALLING CARDS

| | | | | |
|---|---|---|---|---|
| Treble Clef | Bass Clef | Time Signature | Whole Note & Whole Rest | Half Note & Half Rest |
| Quarter Note & Quarter Rest | Eighth Note & Eighth Rest | Dotted Half Note | Staccato | Tie |
| Sharp | Flat | Natural | Bar Line | Fermata |
| Forte | Piano | Crescendo | Decrescendo or Diminuendo | Repeat |

# TIC-TAC-SYMBOLS
## GAME CARD #1

# TIC-TAC-SYMBOLS
## GAME CARD #2

# TIC-TAC-SYMBOLS
## GAME CARD #3

# TIC-TAC-SYMBOLS
## GAME CARD #4

# TIC-TAC-SYMBOLS
## GAME CARD #5

# TIC-TAC-SYMBOLS
## GAME CARD #6

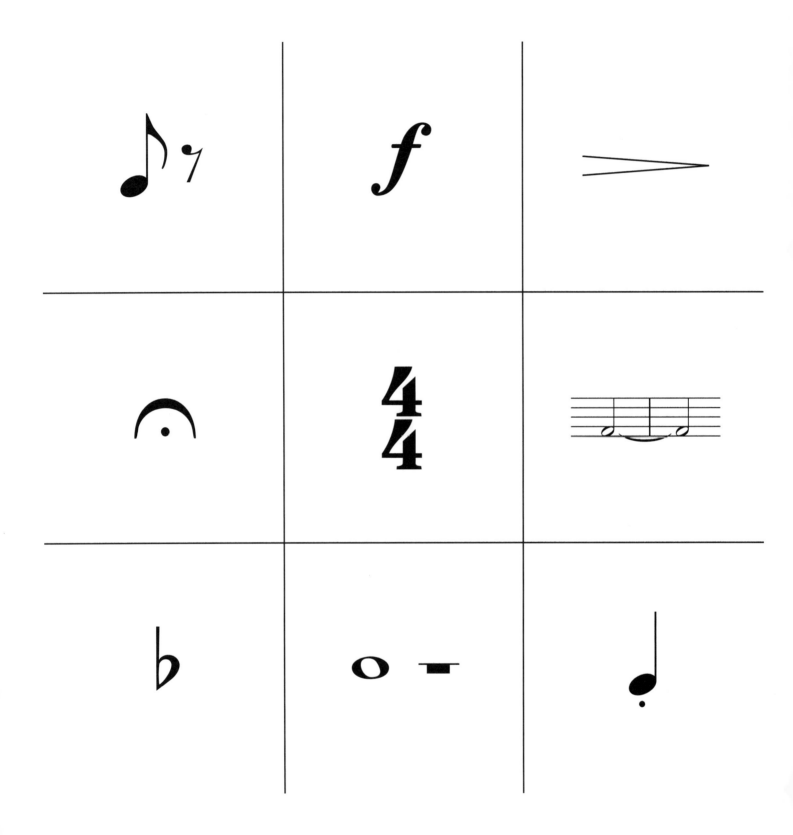

# TIC-TAC-SYMBOLS
## GAME CARD #7

| | | |
|---|---|---|
| $p$ | ♭ | < |
| $\frac{4}{4}$ | 𝄢 | ♪ 𝄾 |
| 𝅗𝅥. | ♮ | 𝄂 |

# TIC-TAC-SYMBOLS
## GAME CARD #8

# TIC-TAC-SYMBOLS
## GAME CARD #9

# TIC-TAC-SYMBOLS
## GAME CARD #10

# TIC-TAC-NOTES MASTER SHEET

| | | | |
|---|---|---|---|
| C | C# | D♭ | D |
| D# | E♭ | E | F |
| F# | G♭ | G | G# |
| A♭ | A | A# | B♭ |
| B | | | |

**DIRECTIONS:** Place note calling cards face down and shuffle or mix. Give a "Tic-Tac-Notes" game card and several tokens to each player. Draw calling cards one at a time. Call out the names of each note and ask players find the corresponding symbol on their game cards. Place the calling card in the corresponding box on the master sheet. The winner is the first player to complete a row in any direction. The winner identifies himself by saying "Tic-Tac-Notes" and he calls back the winning notes for verification. **BONUS:** Each card has two notes that are enharmonic. Finding these could be an additional activity.

# TIC-TAC-NOTES CALLING CARDS

| C | C# | D♭ | D |
|---|----|----|---|
| D# | E♭ | E | F |
| F# | G♭ | G | G# |
| A♭ | A | A# | B♭ |
| B | | | |

# TIC-TAC-NOTES
## GAME CARD #1

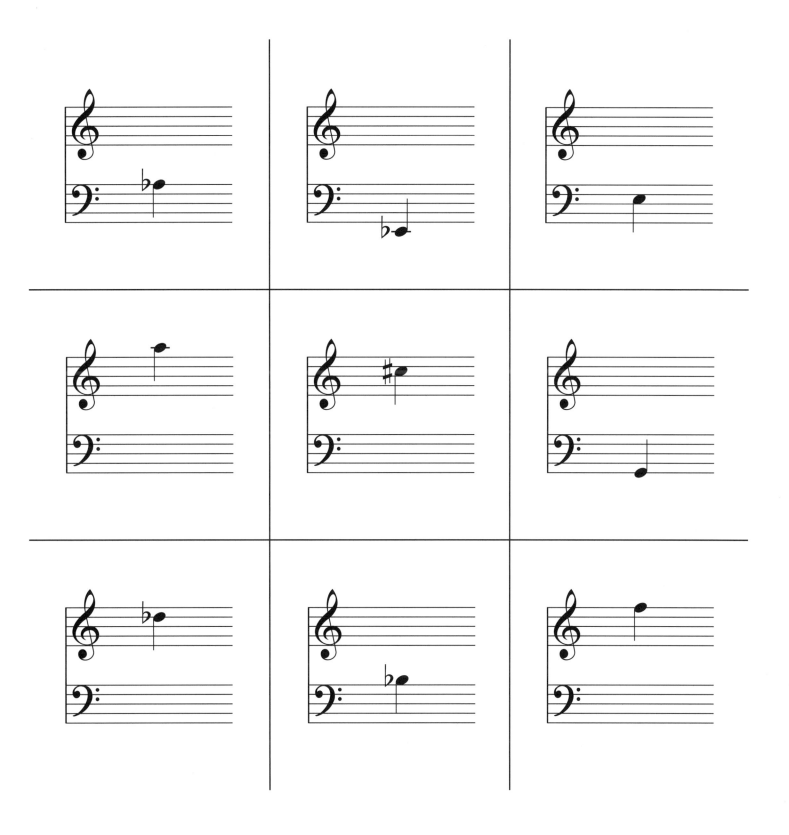

# TIC-TAC-NOTES
## GAME CARD #2

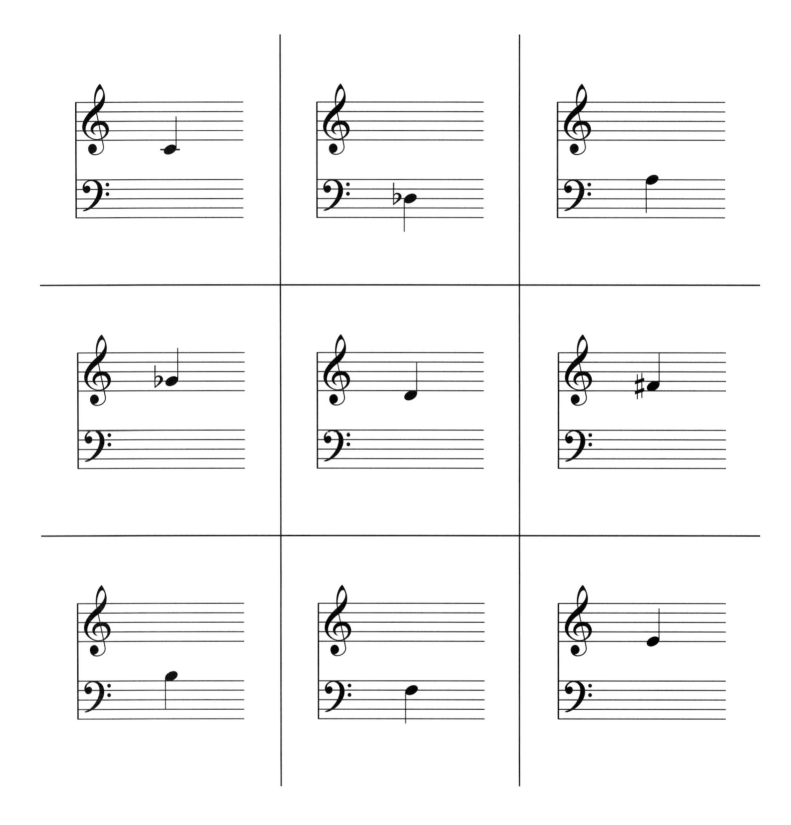

# TIC-TAC-NOTES
## GAME CARD #3

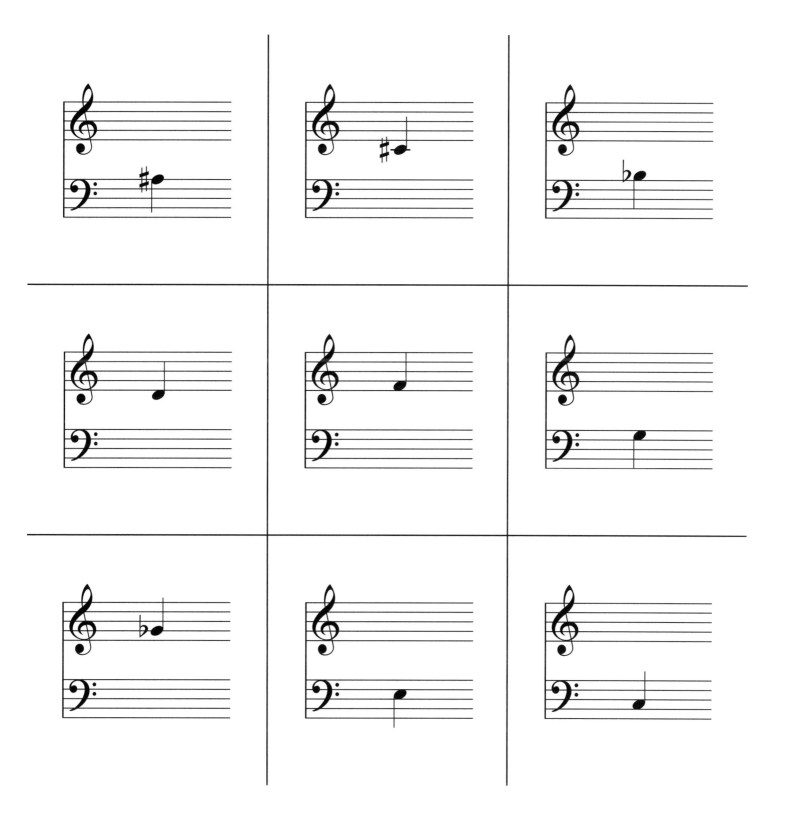

# TIC-TAC-NOTES
## GAME CARD #4

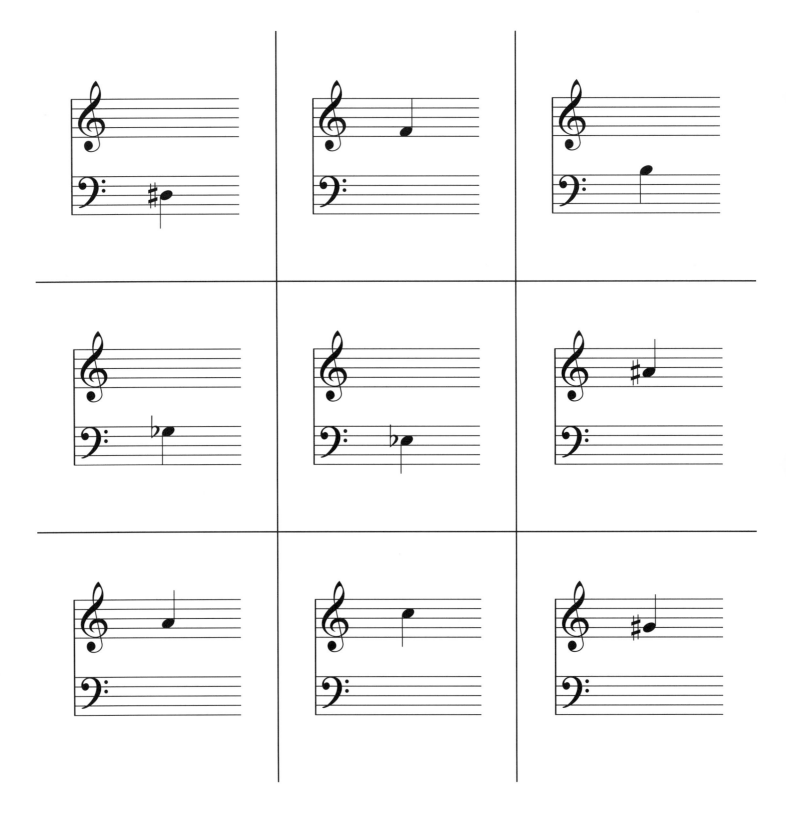

# TIC-TAC-NOTES
## GAME CARD #5

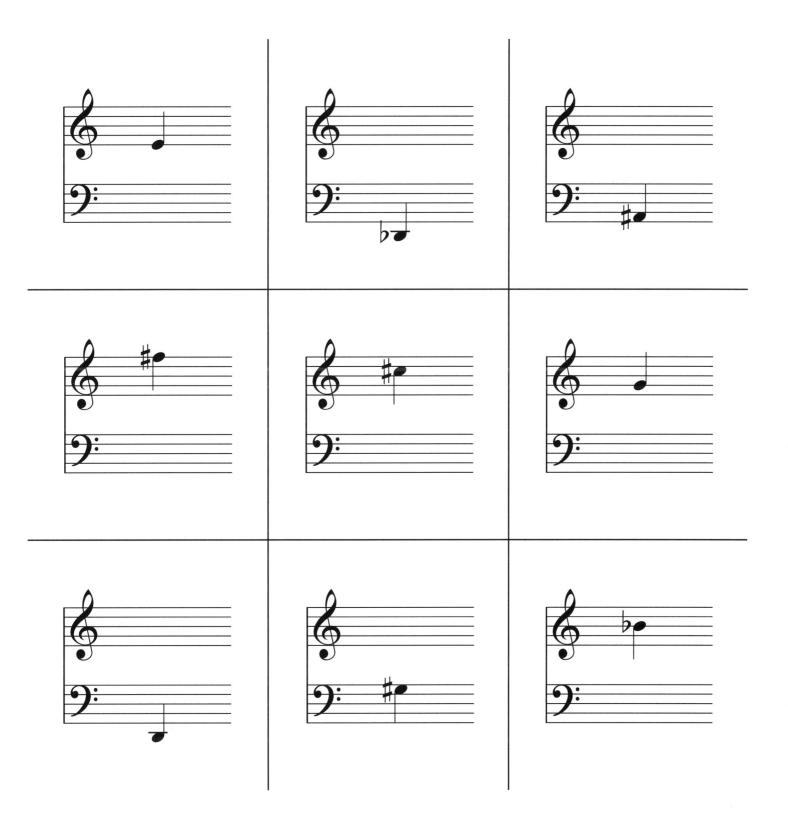

# TIC-TAC-NOTES
## GAME CARD #6

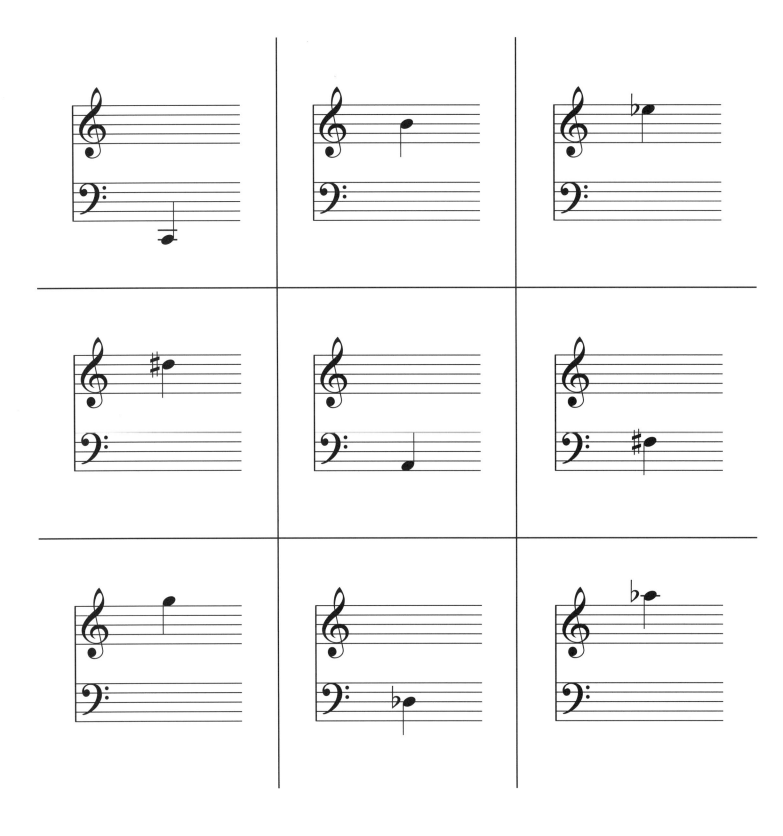

# TIC-TAC-NOTES
## GAME CARD #7

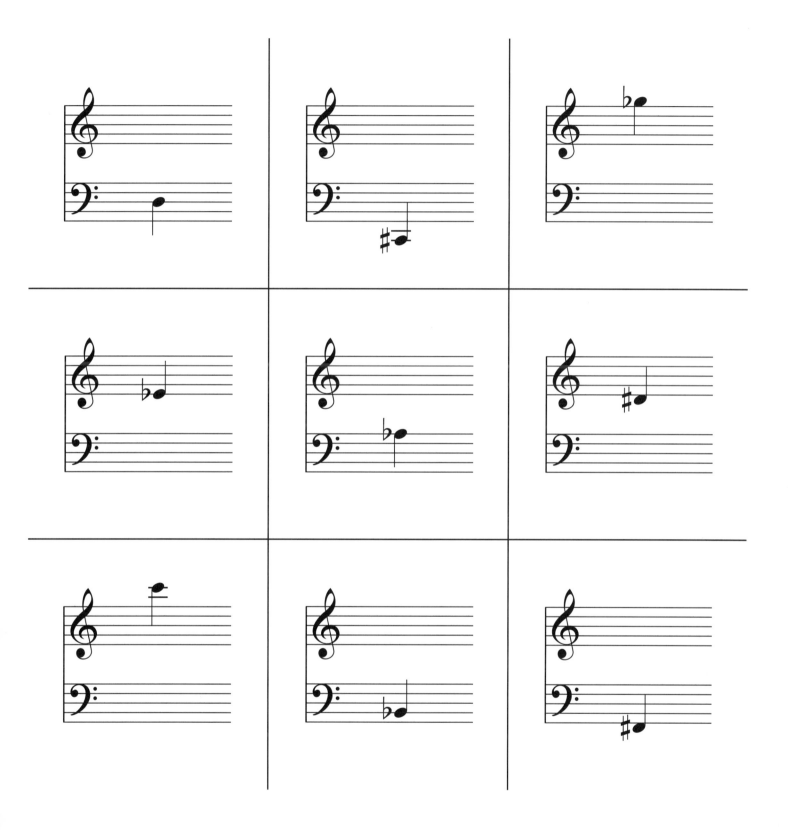

# TIC-TAC-NOTES
## GAME CARD #8

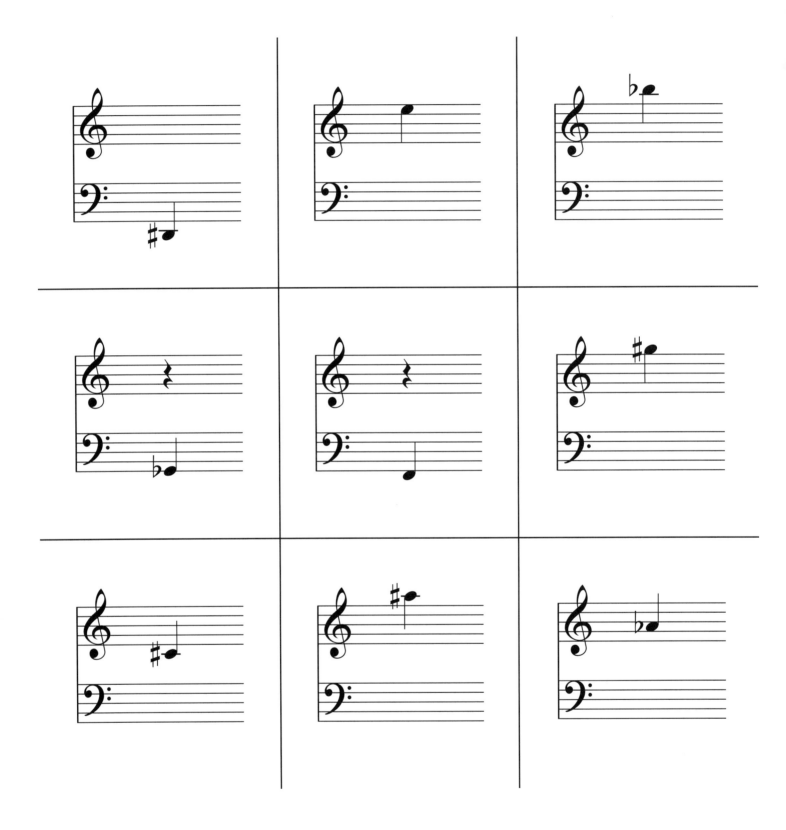

# TIC-TAC-NOTES
## GAME CARD #9

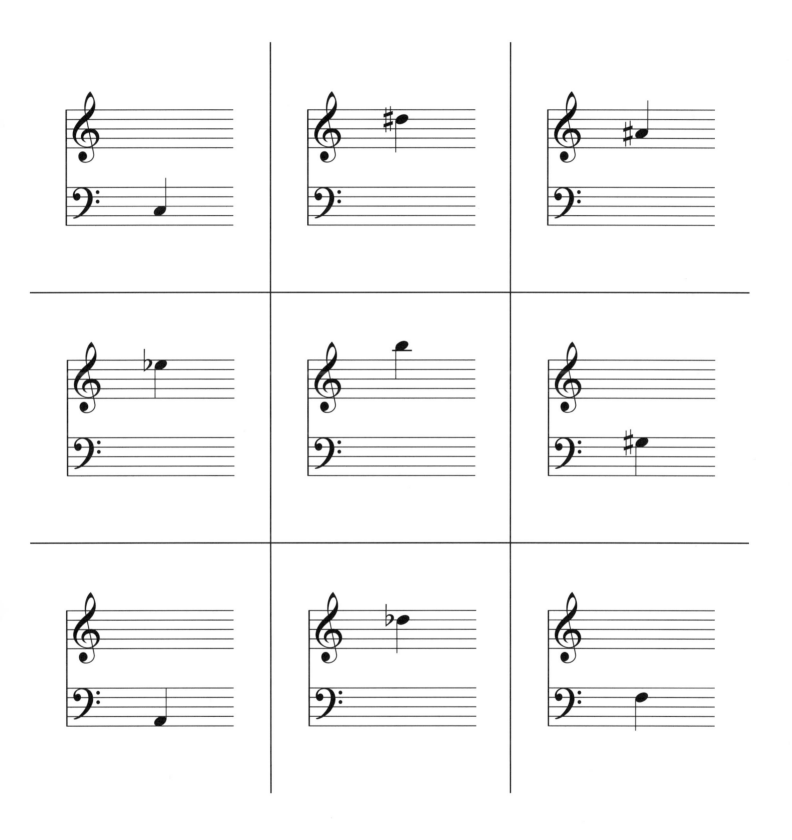

# TIC-TAC-NOTES
## GAME CARD #10

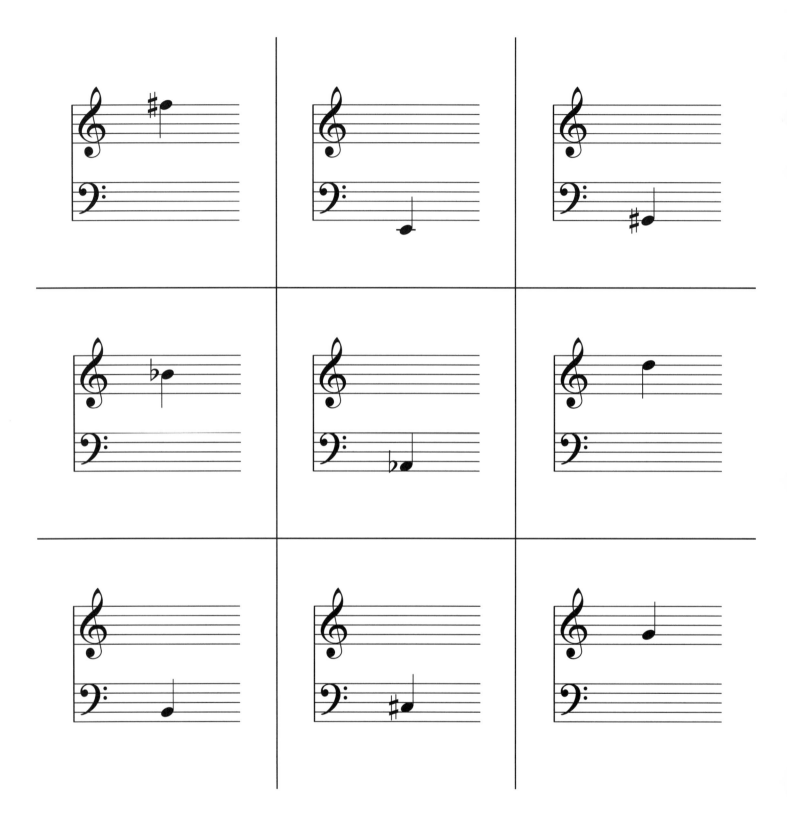

# TIC-TAC-RHYTHM MASTER SHEET

**DIRECTIONS:** Place symbol calling cards face down and shuffle or mix. Give a "Tic-Tac-Rhythm" game card and several tokens to each player. Draw calling cards one at a time. Clap or play the rhythm on a percussion instrument. Players find the corresponding rhythm on their game cards. Place the calling card in the corresponding box on the master sheet. The winner is the first player to complete a row in any direction. The winner identifies himself by saying "Tic-Tac-Rhythm" and he calls back the winning rhythms for verification. **SUGGESTIONS: 1)** For beginning students, hand out copies of the master sheet and review the rhythms before playing the game. **2)** Set the tempo by counting aloud **3)** Use the game as a dictation game. Tap the rhythms and ask students to write the rhythm they hear. **4)** For more than ten players, copy various cards as needed.

# TIC-TAC-RHYTHM CALLING CARDS

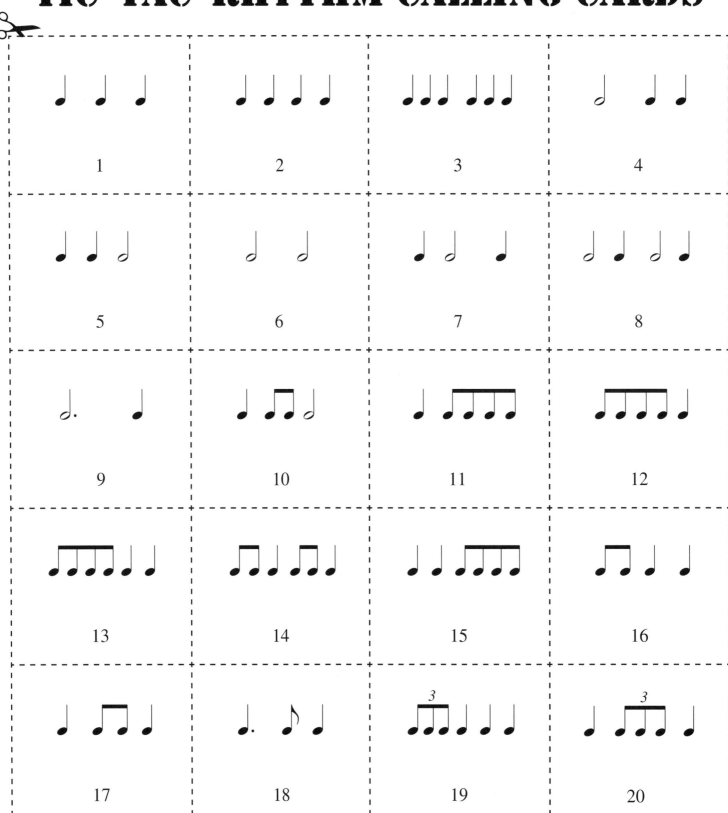

# TIC-TAC-RHYTHM
## GAME CARD #1

# TIC-TAC-RHYTHM
## GAME CARD #2

# TIC-TAC-RHYTHM
## GAME CARD #3

# TIC-TAC-RHYTHM
## GAME CARD #4

# TIC-TAC-RHYTHM
## GAME CARD #5

# TIC-TAC-RHYTHM
## GAME CARD #6

# TIC-TAC-RHYTHM
## GAME CARD #7

# TIC-TAC-RHYTHM
## GAME CARD #8

# TIC-TAC-RHYTHM
## GAME CARD #9

# TIC-TAC-RHYTHM
## GAME CARD #10

# TIC-TAC-INTERVALS MASTER SHEET

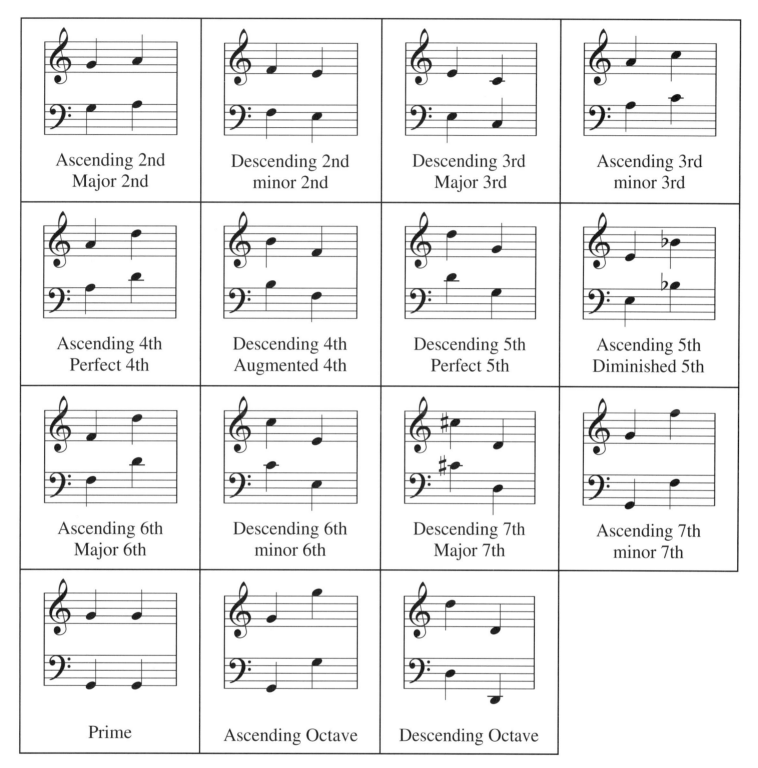

| | | | |
|---|---|---|---|
| Ascending 2nd<br>Major 2nd | Descending 2nd<br>minor 2nd | Descending 3rd<br>Major 3rd | Ascending 3rd<br>minor 3rd |
| Ascending 4th<br>Perfect 4th | Descending 4th<br>Augmented 4th | Descending 5th<br>Perfect 5th | Ascending 5th<br>Diminished 5th |
| Ascending 6th<br>Major 6th | Descending 6th<br>minor 6th | Descending 7th<br>Major 7th | Ascending 7th<br>minor 7th |
| Prime | Ascending Octave | Descending Octave | |

**DIRECTIONS: Play Tic-Tac-Intervals by calling either the direction or the quality of each interval.** Place interval calling cards face down and shuffle or mix. Give a "Tic-Tac-Intervals" game card and several tokens to each player. Draw calling cards one at a time. Call out the direction or the quality of the interval; players find the corresponding interval on their game cards. Place the calling card in the corresponding box on the master sheet. The winner is the first player to complete a row in any direction. The winner identifies himself by saying "Tic-Tac-Intervals" and he calls back the winning notes for verification.

# TIC-TAC-INTERVALS CALLING CARDS

| | | | |
|---|---|---|---|
| Ascending 2nd<br>Major 2nd | Descending 2nd<br>minor 2nd | Descending 3rd<br>Major 3rd | Ascending 3rd<br>minor 3rd |
| Ascending 4th<br>Perfect 4th | Descending 4th<br>Augmented 4th | Descending 5th<br>Perfect 5th | Ascending 5th<br>Diminished 5th |
| Ascending 6th<br>Major 6th | Descending 6th<br>minor 6th | Descending 7th<br>Major 7th | Ascending 7th<br>minor 7th |
| Prime | Ascending Octave | Descending Octave | |

# TIC-TAC-INTERVALS
## GAME CARD #1

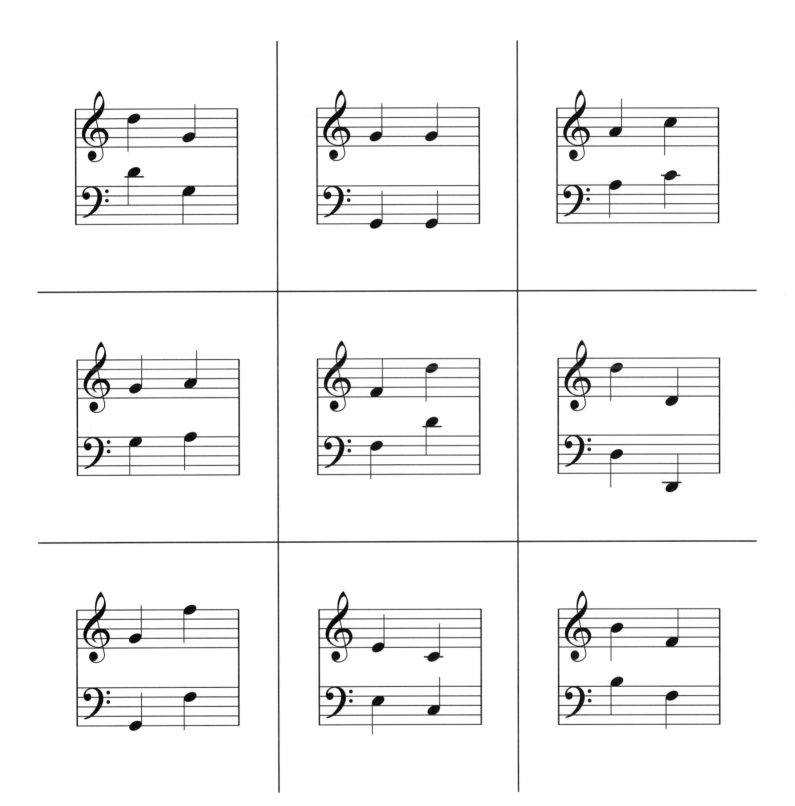

# TIC-TAC-INTERVALS
## GAME CARD #2

# TIC-TAC-INTERVALS
## GAME CARD #3

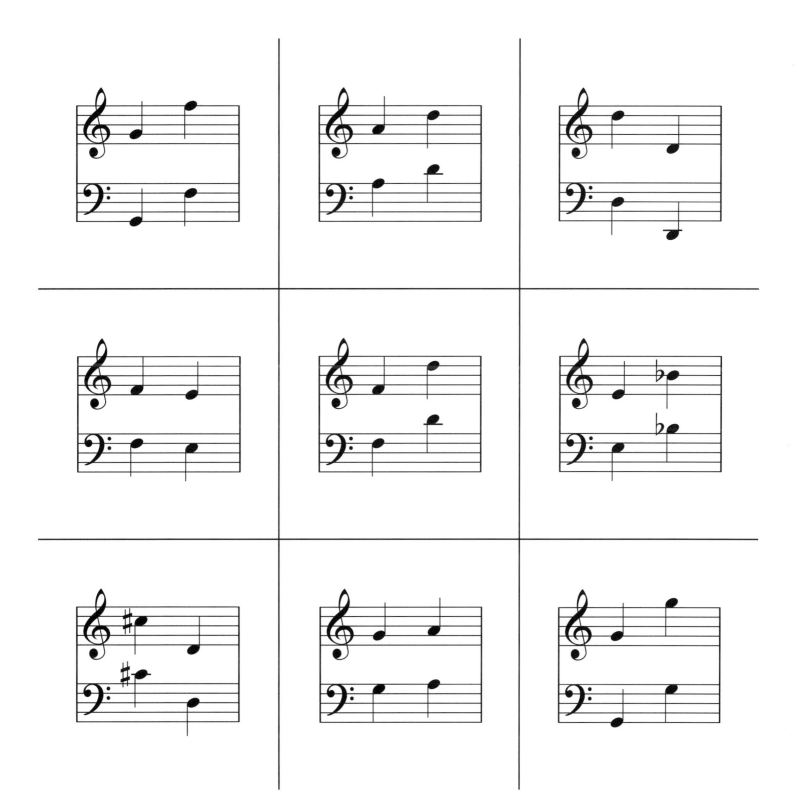

# TIC-TAC-INTERVALS
## GAME CARD #4

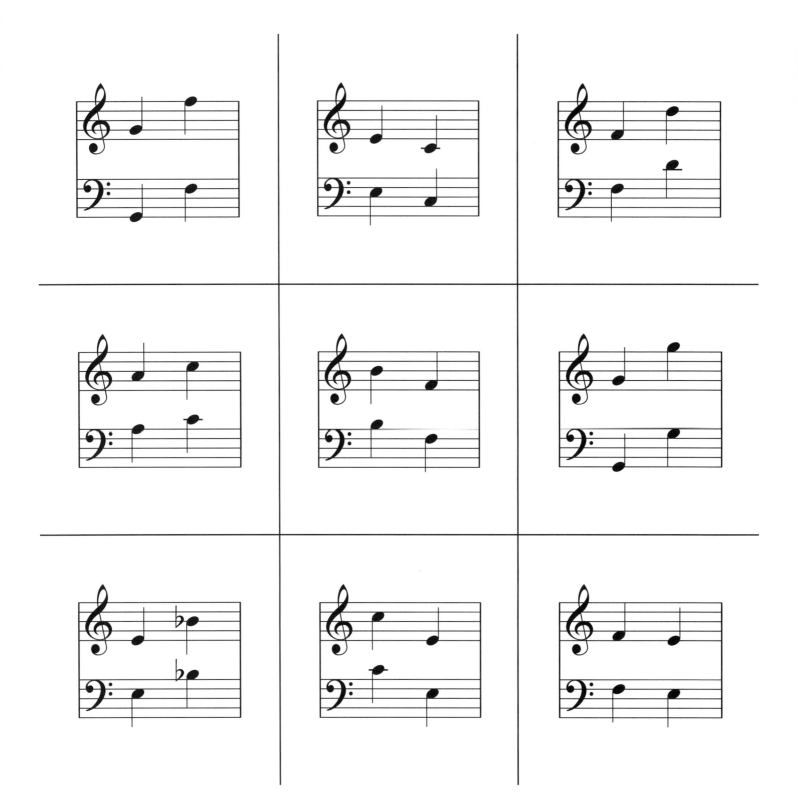

# TIC-TAC-INTERVALS

## GAME CARD #5

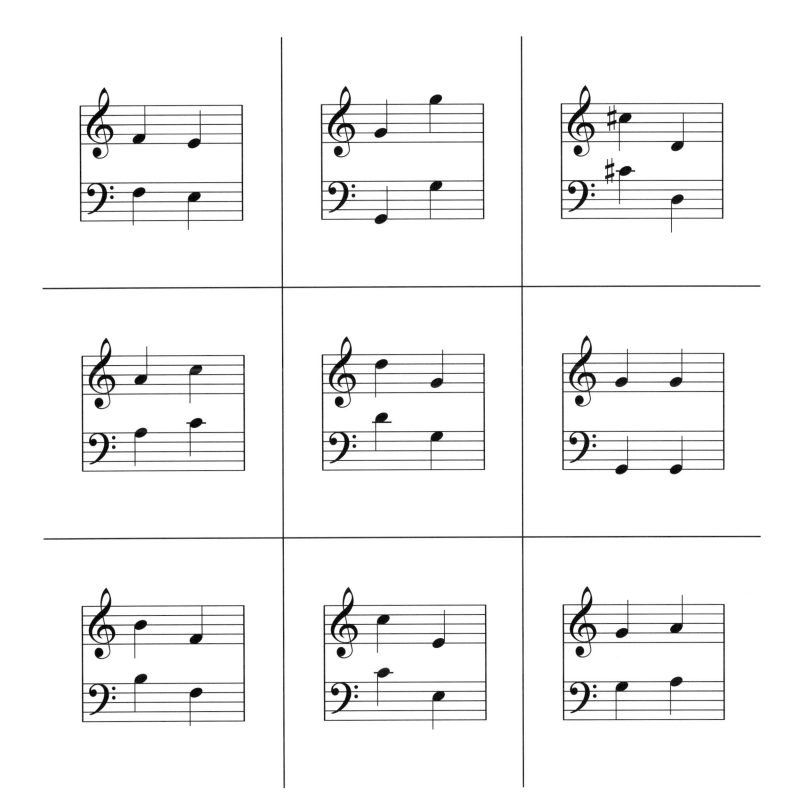

# TIC-TAC-INTERVALS
## GAME CARD #6

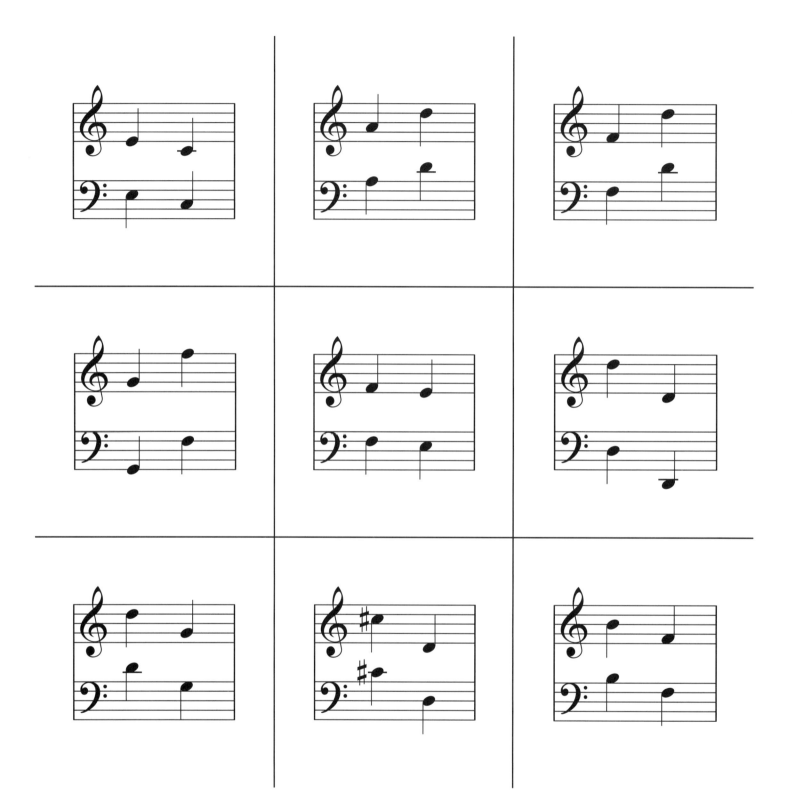

# TIC-TAC-INTERVALS
## GAME CARD #7

# TIC-TAC-INTERVALS
## GAME CARD #8

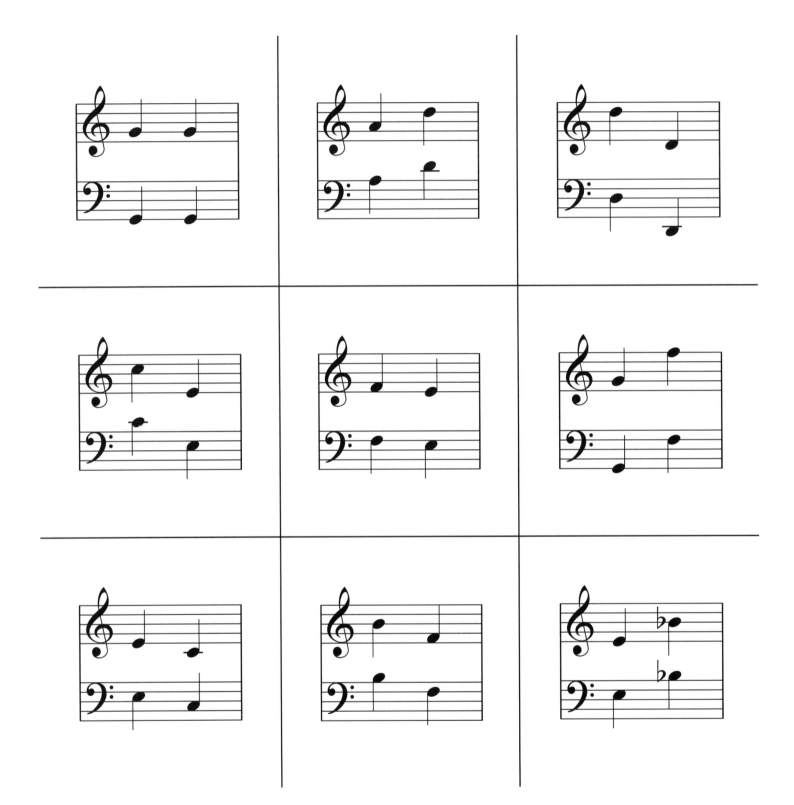

# TIC-TAC-INTERVALS
## GAME CARD #9

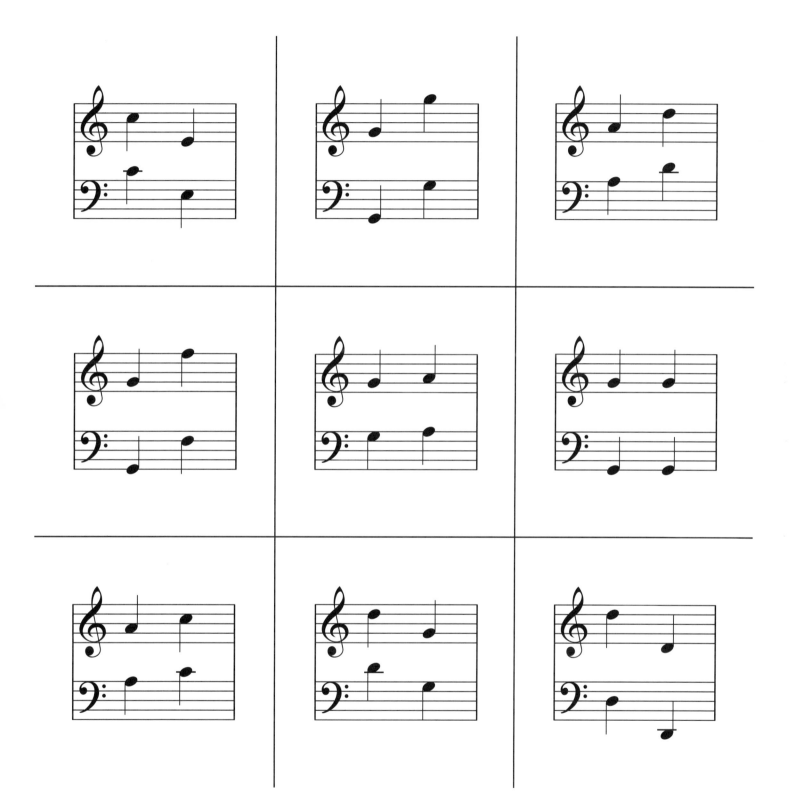

# TIC-TAC-INTERVALS
## GAME CARD #10

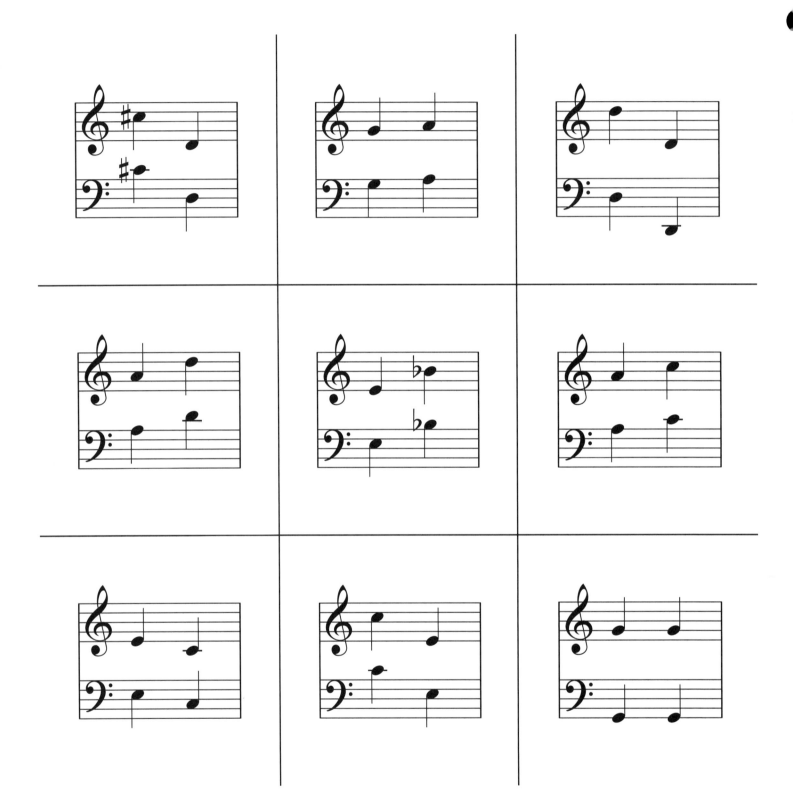

# TIC-TAC-KEYS MASTER SHEET

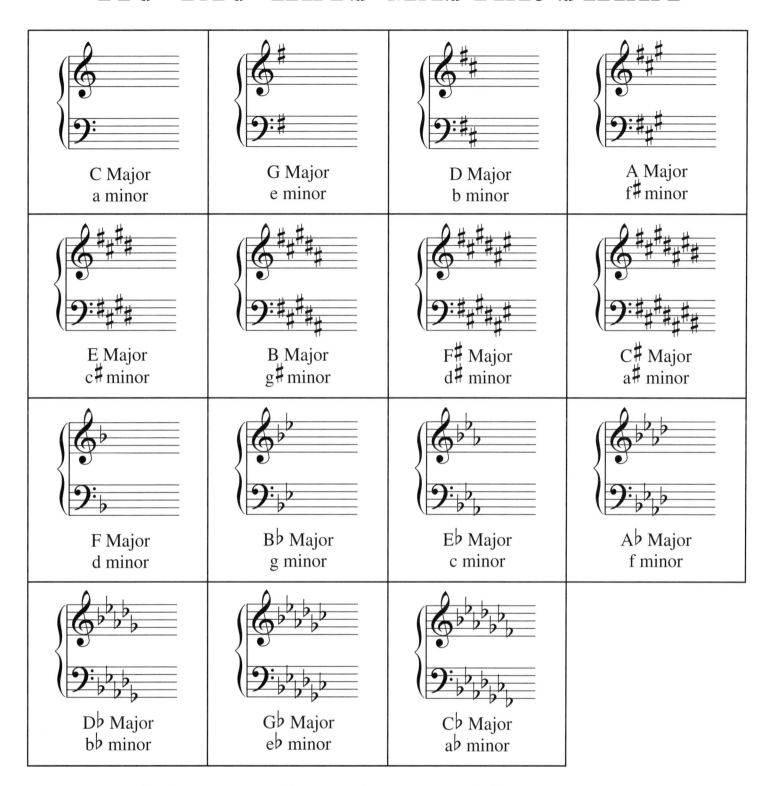

**DIRECTIONS:** Place key signature calling cards face down and shuffle or mix. Give a "Tic-Tac-Keys" game card and several tokens to each player. Draw calling cards one at a time. Call out a major key, minor key, or both; players find the corresponding key signature on their game cards. Place the calling card in the corresponding box on the master sheet. The winner is the first player to complete a row in any direction. The winner identifies himself by saying "Tic-Tac-Keys" and he calls back the winning keys for verification.

# TIC-TAC-KEYS CALLING CARDS

54

# TIC-TAC-KEYS
## GAME CARD #1

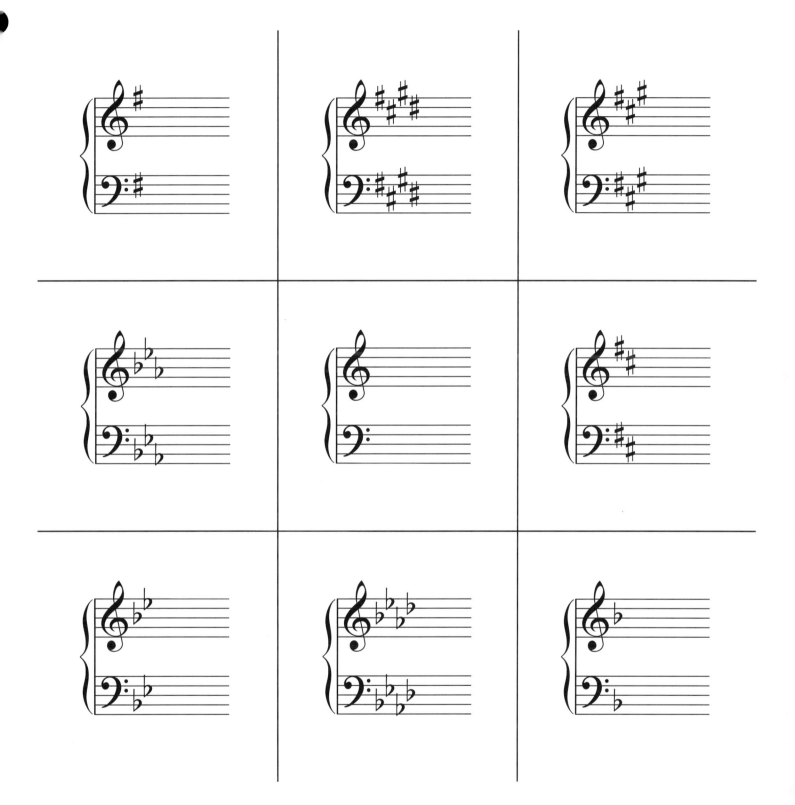

# TIC-TAC-KEYS
## GAME CARD #2

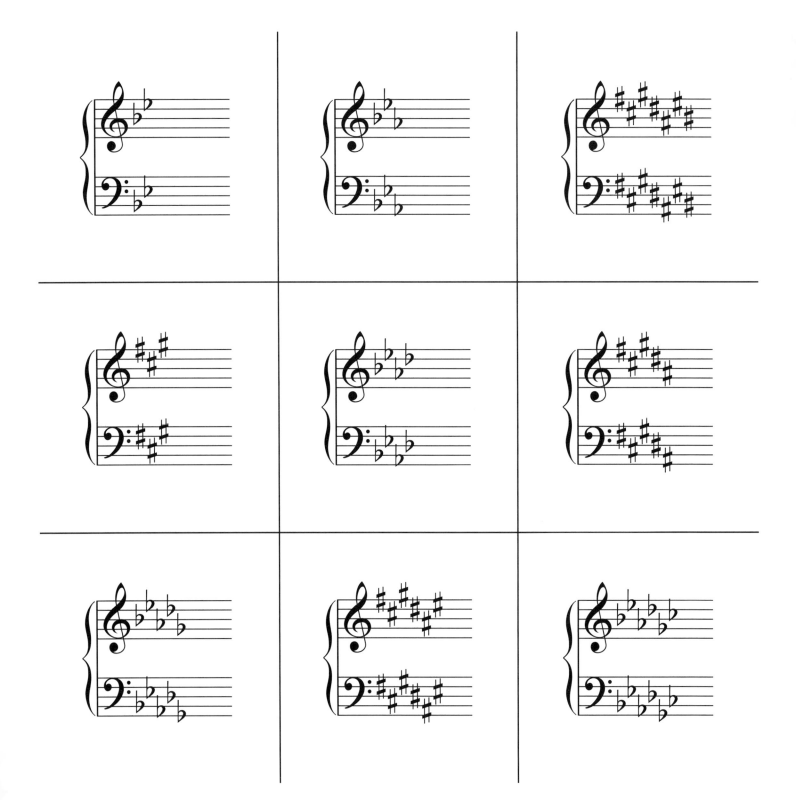

# TIC-TAC-KEYS
## GAME CARD #3

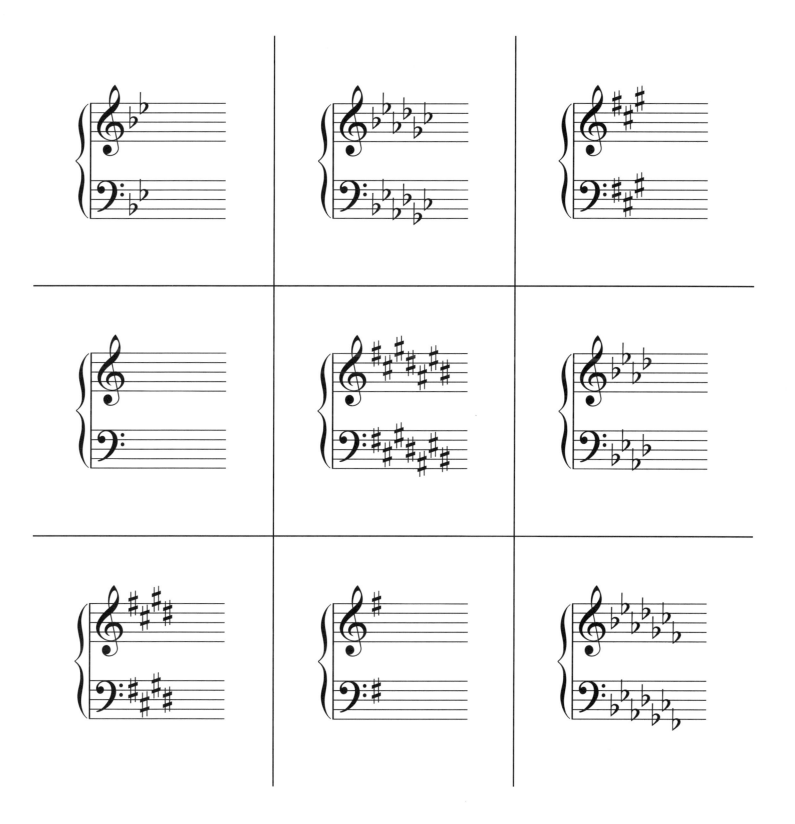

# TIC-TAC-KEYS
## GAME CARD #4

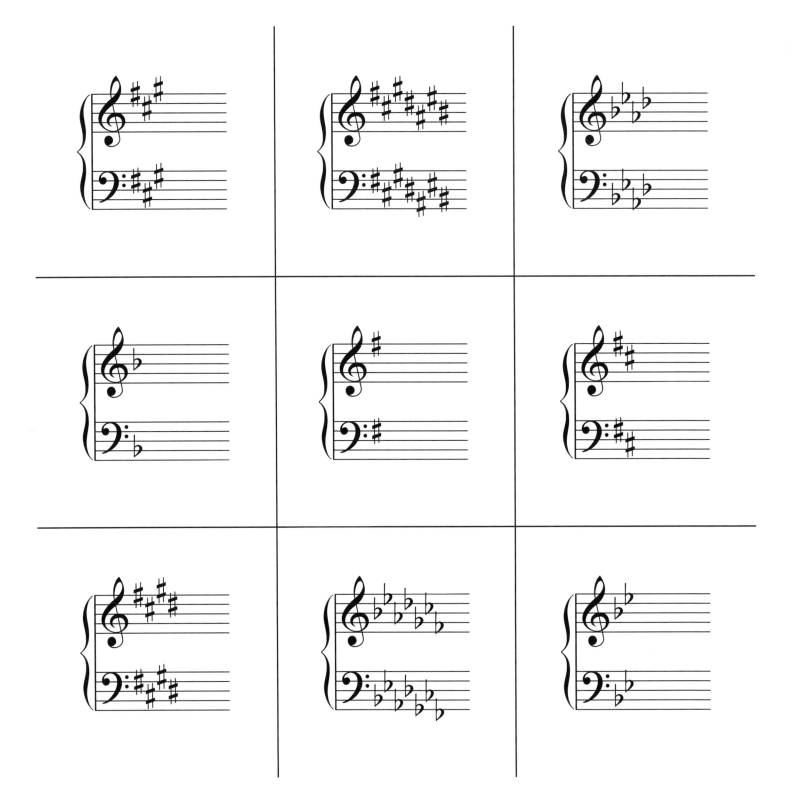

# TIC-TAC-KEYS
## GAME CARD #5

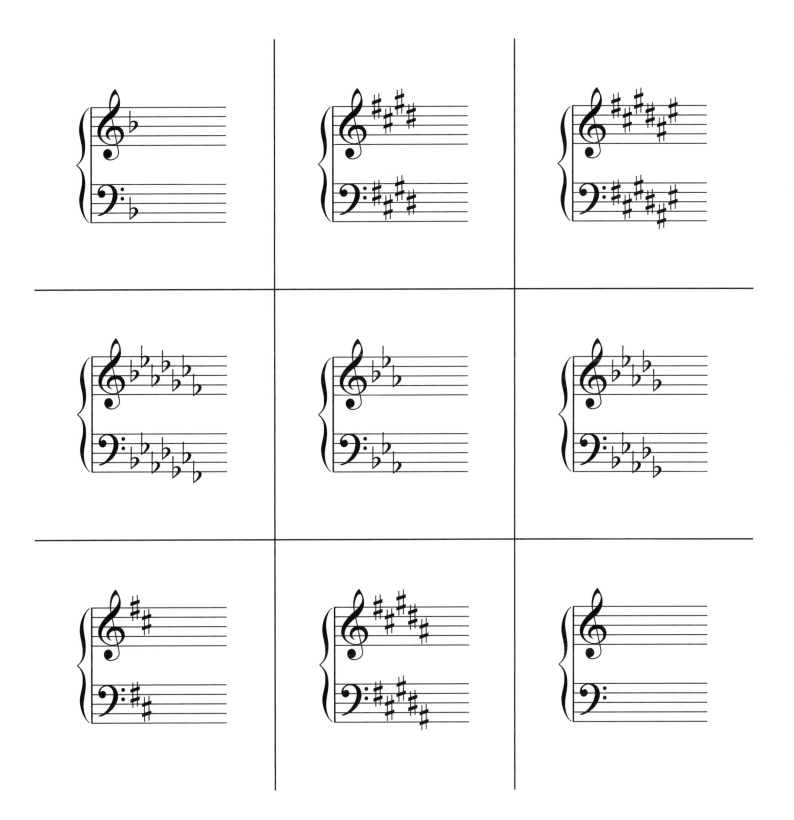

# TIC-TAC-KEYS
## GAME CARD #6

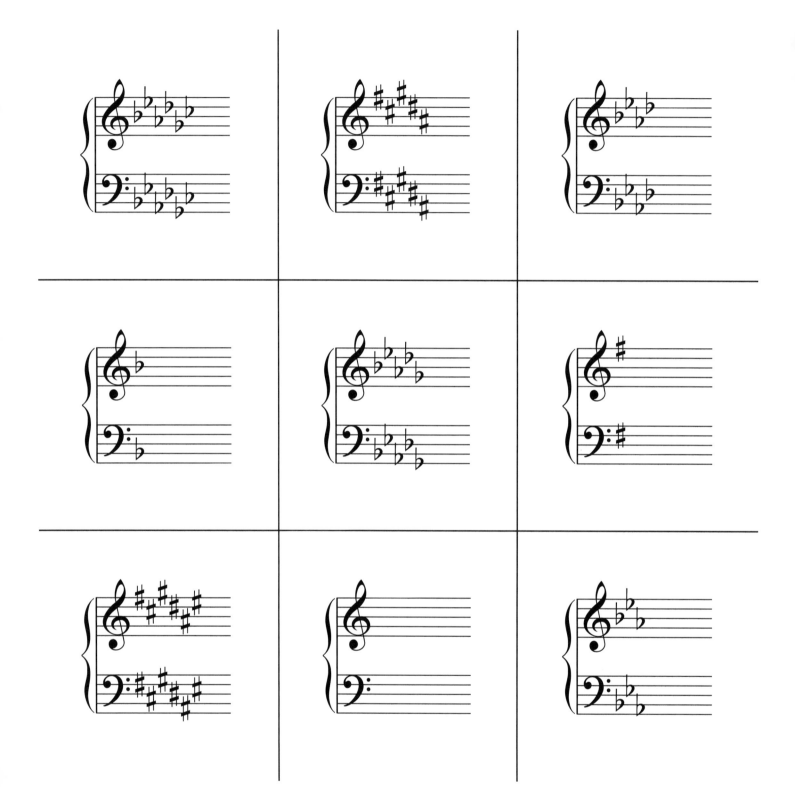

# TIC-TAC-KEYS
## GAME CARD #7

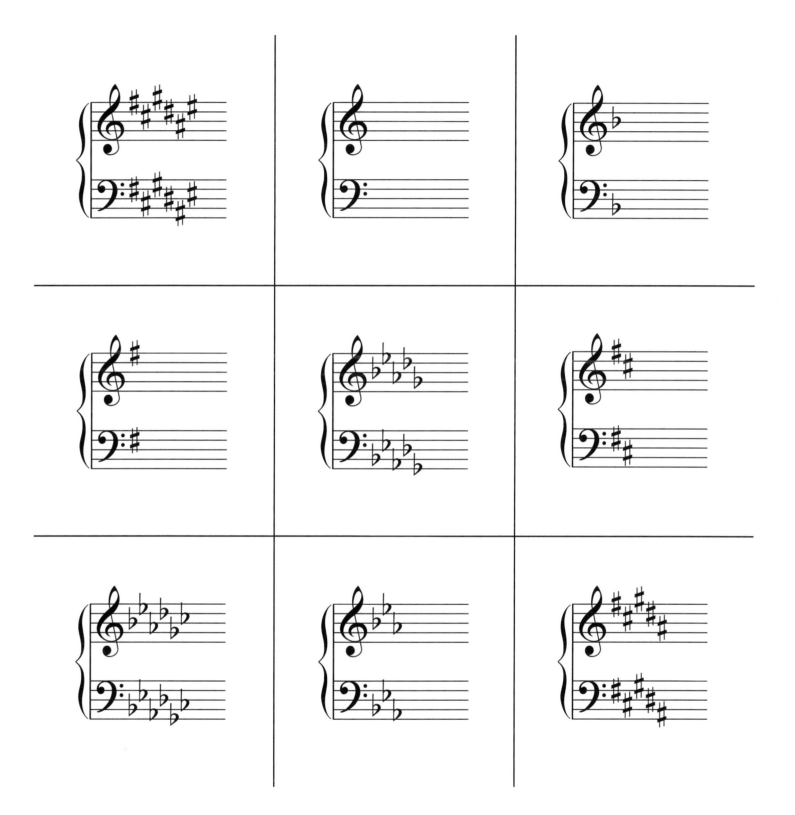

# TIC-TAC-KEYS
## GAME CARD #8

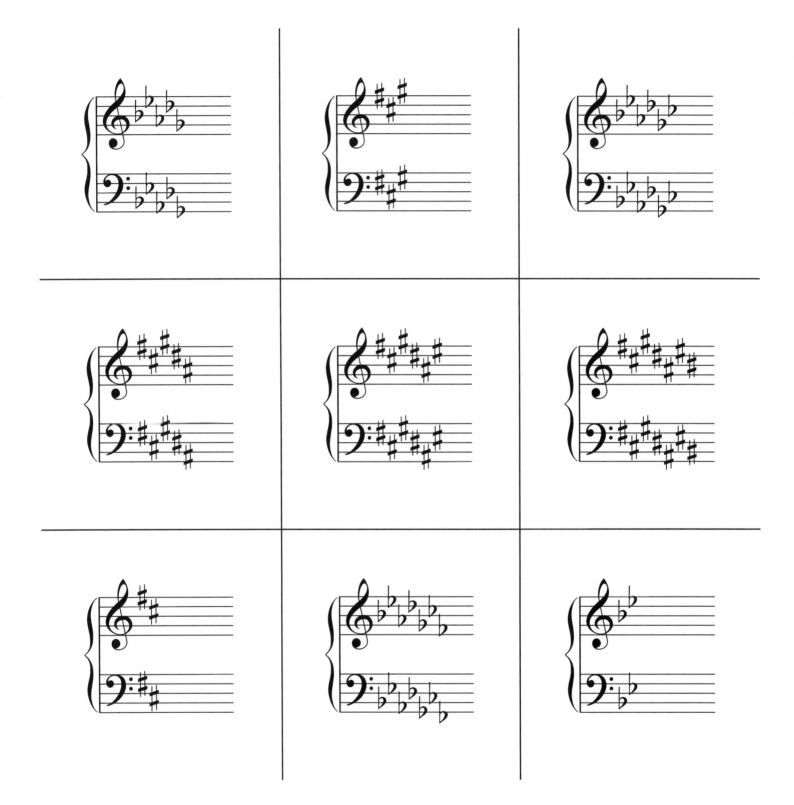

# TIC-TAC-KEYS
## GAME CARD #9

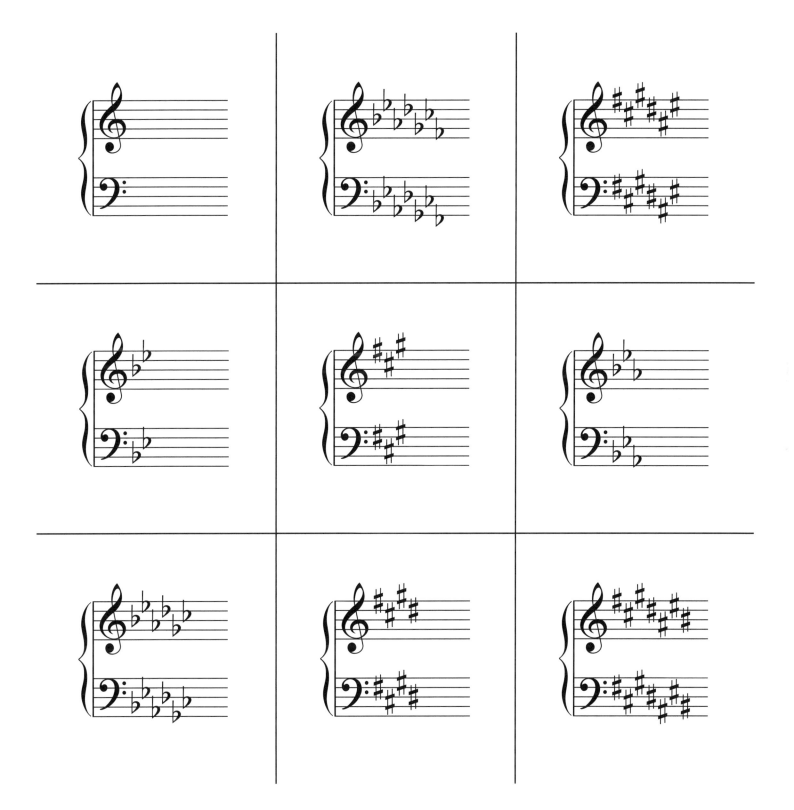

# TIC-TAC-KEYS
## GAME CARD #10

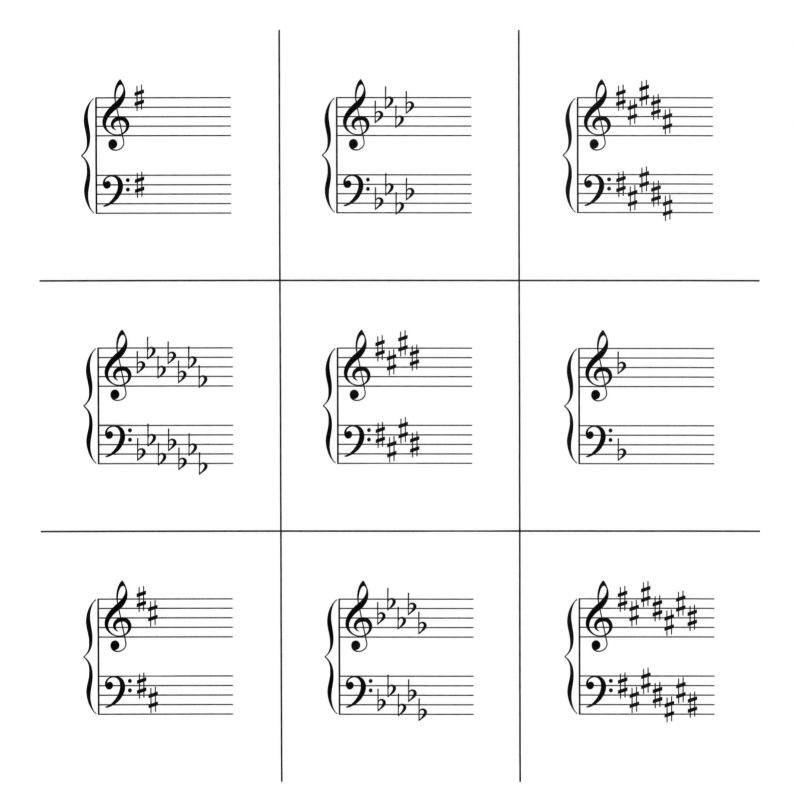

# TIC-TAC-TEMPOS MASTER SHEET

| | | | |
|---|---|---|---|
| **Grave**<br><br>Solemn, serious, very slow. | **Largo**<br><br>MM 40-48<br><br>Broad, very slow. | **Lento**<br><br>MM 48-56<br><br>Slow, slower than Adagio. | **Adagio**<br><br>MM 58-69<br><br>At ease, slow. |
| **Allegro**<br><br>MM 120-132<br><br>Fast, cheerful, quick. | **Allegretto**<br><br>MM 100-116<br><br>Moderately quick tempo. | **Moderato**<br><br>MM 84-96<br><br>Moderate, medium tempo. | **Andante**<br><br>MM 72-80<br><br>Slow, walking tempo. |
| **Vivace**<br><br>MM 138-168<br><br>Lively, brisk. | **Presto**<br><br>MM 176-192<br><br>Very fast. | **Prestissimo**<br><br>As fast as possible. | **Ritardando**<br><br>Gradually slower. |
| **Rubato**<br><br>Robbed time; expressive variation of tempo. | **Meno Mosso**<br><br>Less motion. | **Più Mosso**<br><br>More motion. | **Acccelerando**<br><br>Gradually faster. |

**DIRECTIONS:** Place tempo calling cards face down and shuffle or mix. Give a "Tic-Tac-Tempos" game card and several tokens to each player. Draw calling cards one at a time. Call out a tempo word, definition or both; players find the corresponding tempo on their game cards. Place the calling card in the corresponding box on the master sheet. The winner is the first player to complete a row in any direction. The winner identifies himself by saying "Tic-Tac-Tempos" and he calls back the winning tempos for verification.

# TIC-TAC-TEMPOS CALLING CARDS

| | | | |
|---|---|---|---|
| **Grave**<br><br>Solemn, serious, very slow. | **Largo**<br><br>MM 40-48<br><br>Broad, very slow. | **Lento**<br><br>MM 48-56<br><br>Slow, slower than Adagio. | **Adagio**<br><br>MM 58-69<br><br>At ease, slow. |
| **Allegro**<br><br>MM 120-132<br><br>Fast, cheerful, quick. | **Allegretto**<br><br>MM 100-116<br><br>Moderately quick tempo. | **Moderato**<br><br>MM 84-96<br><br>Moderate, medium tempo. | **Andante**<br><br>MM 72-80<br><br>Slow, walking tempo. |
| **Vivace**<br><br>MM 138-168<br><br>Lively, brisk. | **Presto**<br><br>MM 176-192<br><br>Very fast. | **Prestissimo**<br><br>As fast as possible. | **Ritardando**<br><br>Gradually slower. |
| **Rubato**<br><br>Robbed time; expressive variation of tempo. | **Meno Mosso**<br><br>Less motion. | **Più Mosso**<br><br>More motion. | **Acccelerando**<br><br>Gradually faster. |

# TIC-TAC-TEMPOS

GAME CARD #1

| | | |
|---|---|---|
| Grave | Allegretto | Vivace |
| Allegro | Più Mosso | Accelerando |
| Adagio | Rubato | Lento |

# TIC-TAC-TEMPOS
## GAME CARD #2

| | | |
|---|---|---|
| Moderato | Largo | Allegro |
| Meno Mosso | Lento | Accelerando |
| Vivace | Più Mosso | Allegretto |

# TIC-TAC-TEMPOS
## GAME CARD #3

| | | |
|---|---|---|
| Largo | Meno Mosso | Accelerando |
| Prestissimo | Vivace | Adagio |
| Moderato | Allegro | Rubato |

# TIC-TAC-TEMPOS
## GAME CARD #4

| | | |
|---|---|---|
| Vivace | Ritardando | Andante |
| Rubato | Largo | Prestissimo |
| Accelerando | Meno Mosso | Grave |

# TIC-TAC-TEMPOS
## GAME CARD #5

| | | |
|---|---|---|
| Lento | Presto | Rubato |
| Allegretto | Ritardando | Grave |
| Largo | Andante | Adagio |

# TIC-TAC-TEMPOS
## GAME CARD #6

| | | |
|---|---|---|
| Allegro | Più Mosso | Moderato |
| Accelerando | Prestissimo | Andante |
| Presto | Adagio | Ritardando |

# TIC-TAC-TEMPOS
## GAME CARD #7

| | | |
|---|---|---|
| Allegretto | Lento | Meno Mosso |
| Più Mosso | Allegro | Largo |
| Adagio | Moderato | Presto |

# TIC-TAC-TEMPOS
## GAME CARD #8

| | | |
|---|---|---|
| Meno Mosso | Andante | Vivace |
| Ritardando | Presto | Moderato |
| Rubato | Grave | Prestissimo |

# TIC-TAC-TEMPOS
## GAME CARD #9

| | | |
|---|---|---|
| Allegretto | Lento | Moderato |
| Meno Mosso | Andante | Rubato |
| Largo | Grave | Presto |

# TIC-TAC-TEMPOS
## GAME CARD #10

| | | |
|---|---|---|
| Andante | Grave | Più Mosso |
| Presto | Allegretto | Lento |
| Ritardando | Vivace | Prestissimo |

# Suggestions for using the "Circle of Keys" and Manuscript Paper

The Circle of Keys and manuscript paper are ideal to use as worksheets before playing the games or at any time the players need to review the various concepts. Here are some suggestions.

## CIRCLE OF KEYS

**Tic-Tac-Symbols** – Ask players to write a symbol on each staff around the circle. Since there are 15 staves and 20 symbols, they can put two symbols on five of the staves. You can ask them to copy the symbols from the master sheet or write them from being called orally.

**Tic-Tac-Notes** – Using two copies of the "Circle," have players write notes on the treble and bass staffs that match the letters around the circle. Since the game uses notes between "Bass C" and "High C" you could have them write all the notes between those two ledger lines.

**Tic-Tac-Rhythm** – On each staff around the circle, ask players to find and write rhythms from the master sheet that equal a designated number of beats. There are rhythms in the game that equal 2, 3 and 4 beats with the quarter note receiving one beat.

**Tic-Tac-Intervals** – Have players draw specified intervals from each tonic, such as a "2nd from each tonic" or a 3rd, 4th , etc. up to an octave. Ask advanced players to write major, minor, or perfect intervals.

**Tic-Tac-Keys** – 1. Using the treble or bass staff, have players write the major key signatures around the circle. 2. Write the relative minor key next to each major key around the circle. 3. Have advanced players write the key signatures for the minor keys.

**Tic-Tac-Tempos** – Using a sheet of plain paper, ask players to write the tempo words and their definitions from the master sheet. They could be tested over the words prior to playing the game.

## MANUSCRIPT PAPER

Let your imagination be your guide. Players may write scales for the key signatures, or even compose a short piece using a rhythm from the game as a motive. All of the suggestions from above can also be done on the manuscript paper.

# CIRCLE OF KEYS

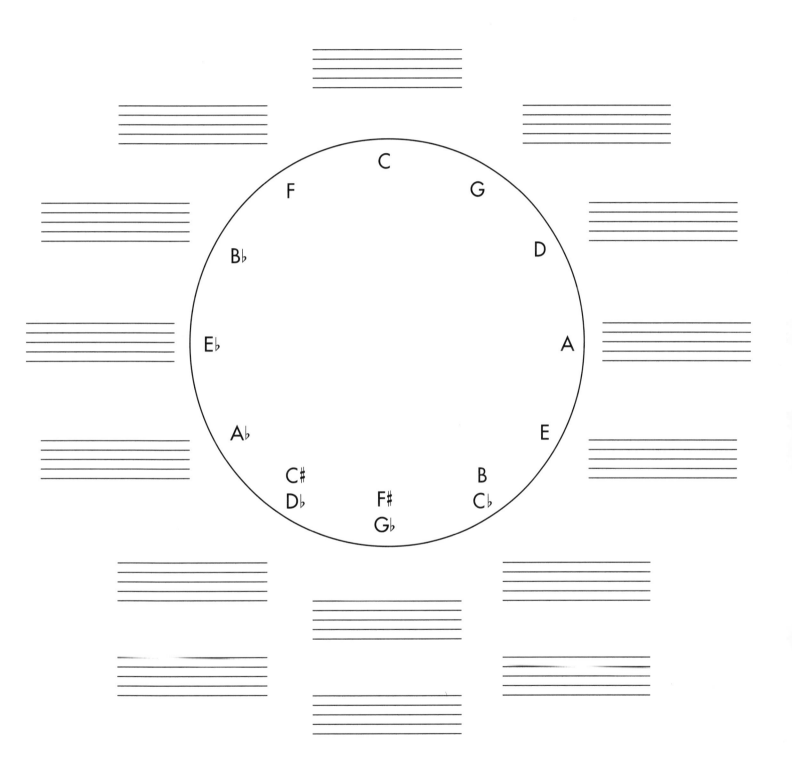

Karen Harrington, NCTM, maintains a private studio with over thirty-five students in Tulsa, Oklahoma, where she has taught piano for twenty-seven years. She is also an Adjunct Professor of Piano at the University of Tulsa. A graduate of the University of Oklahoma, she holds a BME degree with piano emphasis. Before opening her independent studio, she taught music in the Tulsa Public Schools for eight years.

Karen served as Music Teachers National Association's South Central Division President and for two years as a member of its national board of directors. She has also been president of Tulsa Accredited Music Teachers Association and is currently Vice President of Oklahoma Music Teachers Association. She has also served OMTA as member of the board of directors, a member of the certification and audition committees, and as Northeast District President. Karen has also been president of the Piano Study Club, a club in Tulsa dating from 1915 for those who want to perform and study the piano. She is a clinician and adjudicator for her state and local associations.

Through her company, Music Games 'N Things, Karen has produced music theory games including *Forward March*, *Time Out*, *Perfect Pitch*, and the *Tic-Tac-Games*. She is a coauthor of the Hal Leonard Student Piano Library Theory Workbooks and author of the Notespellers.